A Mother's Journey

Finding Faith & Hope After Loss

By Patricia Poindexter

A Mother's Journey
© 2025 Patricia Poindexter

Published by Starlily Publishing
Imprint of Dearverse Media Productions
San Antonio, TX

For information, permissions, or inquiries, please contact: info@dearversemedia.com

ISBN: 979-8-9926781-2-3

Editor: Bambina Dear
Cover Photo: The Rock San Antonio

About Dearverse Media Productions

Dearverse Media Productions is an independent storytelling house dedicated to crafting immersive narratives across multiple art forms. Founded by Bambina Dear, we specialize in evocative, thought-provoking stories that blend genres, visual art, and cinematic storytelling.

At Dearverse, we believe that stories have the power to shape worlds, both on the page and on the screen. Our mission is to create deeply resonant works that challenge, inspire, and connect audiences through bold, unconventional storytelling.

Dedication

First in My Life

Father, I am finally able to tell my story.
I experienced my worst day on September 24, 2017. The day I lost my youngest child, Andre, I thought I had lost myself too.

It has been years now, and it is only by Your grace that I am still here.
   - Pat

To My Children and Grandchildren

To Paula, Desiree, and Dominique:
You have walked through the same pain of losing your brother. Even with broken hearts and with a broken mama, you pulled together. You made the calls, greeted family and friends who came to offer condolences, and faced the hardest task of all, planning your brother's service. I love you more than words can ever say. Thank you for holding me up when you yourselves were in pain.

To Chelsea, Miracle, Teegan, Dredai, and Dakari:
Omi loves you more than you can imagine. You bring happiness and laughter back into our family. Dredai, your father named you in memory of your uncle Andre, and I know Andre would have been so proud of you.

I will never forget a holiday a few years ago. As we prayed and gave thanks for the meal, the family, and those no longer with us, your small voice spoke up: "And Andre!" When we looked at you, you simply added, "Andre's here."

In your innocence and purity, you reminded us that love lives on. Grandchildren are a blessing. Each of you is my answered prayer, and I cover you daily in prayer.

Acknowledgments and Thanks

I want to thank my pastors, Apostle Kevin Duhart, Pastor Lisa Duhart, and The Rock San Antonio family for your prayers, flowers, cards, and food.

Thank you to Rev. Claude Axel and the Mt. Pilgrim Baptist Church family in Corpus Christi. This was Andre's home church, where he accepted Jesus as Lord and Savior, baptized by Rev. Axel alongside his brother. Thank you for opening your doors to us during such a painful time.

To my former coworkers at Kohl's, thank you for your kindness, your signed card, your gifts, and for allowing me the time I needed.

To my Navy Army Credit Union (now Rally Credit Union) family, your presence and love meant so much.

To my brothers and sisters in law, Richard and Bert, Jimmy and Nicci, and to my daughter DeDe: Thank you is not enough, but I mean it with all my heart.

To Andre's brother Eugene, this surely was not what the siblings had in mind when planning a get together. I wish you had all been able to visit as you dreamed, but God knows best.

To those who traveled miles to be with us, I am forever grateful.

Isaiah 57:1
The righteous perish, and no one lays it to heart. Merciful men are taken away, and no one considers that the righteous is taken away from the evil.

Table of Contents

Introduction

Dear Reader,

I pray that by sharing my journey, you will find a sense of hope for your own.

The loss of my son was sudden and unexpected. Andre was killed in a senseless car accident on September 24, 2017. No parent is ever prepared to bury their child. In that moment, I had to grow in ways I never thought possible.

Even in his death, I experienced a miracle. God answers prayers, though not always in the way we expect. Satan meant to destroy me, but God turned even this tragedy into something that would bring Him glory.

In these pages, I share my tears, my heartache, and the countless nights on my knees praying. I cried out to God's promises when I felt too weak to stand. There were moments when I almost gave up. That's exactly what the enemy wanted, but I held on. If I gave up, who would cover my children in prayer?

When I say grief is a journey, I mean it. I went from praying in desperation, to demanding that Satan release his grip on my family, to finally surrendering everything to God.

I used to look into Andre's eyes and see the battle stirring in his soul. His hugs grew tighter, as though he wanted to hold on but didn't know how. I prayed daily for God to touch his heart and remind him who he belonged to.

It is not a one-time prayer for our children. It is a daily fight. We must pray when we feel strong, and we must pray when we are too weak to speak.

Even now, when people ask me how many children I have, I always answer: "I have four. My youngest is deceased." I will never leave Andre out of my story.

The last time we were together was for my niece's wedding. It was a joyful night filled with cousins, laughter, and celebration. None of us imagined that just two months later Andre would be gone. That evening, he apologized to people he had hurt, mended his relationship with his father, and smiled more beautifully than I had ever seen him smile. Looking back, I believe he was getting his house in order.

I serve a living God. A God of second and third chances. He heard the prayers of my mother and father, who raised eight children in church. And I know He hears my prayers for my children and grandchildren.

This book is my testimony: that grief is real, that healing is possible, and that God is faithful. My hope is that it will comfort you in your own storm and remind you that you are not alone.

From Grief to Depression

It was a Sunday morning like any other, or so I thought. It was still dark outside on **September 24, 2017**, when thunderous banging rattled the front door and jolted me from sleep. My daughter walked down the hallway, hesitant. I met her in the living room just as my oldest son burst through the door, tears streaming down his face. I searched my daughter's eyes for answers; hers were filled with the same terror.

"Mama, I'm so sorry. It's Andre. He's been in an accident... he's gone."

Everything stopped.

At 2:30 a.m. my baby was in a hit and run motorcycle accident. At 3:30 a.m. he took his last breath while I was sleeping, unaware that my child was leaving this world. My mind refused to accept it. *God, what are they saying? Are You hearing this?* Questions pummeled me: *Was he scared? Was he in pain? Did he call out for me?* I will never know. I only knew that losing him tore a hole in me I didn't believe could exist.

I was not ready to say goodbye, but God does not ask for our input. Suddenly I was expected to live daily without my child. I was expected to think rationally, to "move forward," to breathe. The despair pressed on my chest like a weight. People say, *"It gets easier."* In those first days I could not bear to hear it. I wanted someone to tell me how to stop the racing thoughts, how to rinse the pain from my bones, how to live as *me* again.

God did not leave me to suffer alone. He understands sorrow because He sent His Son, Jesus, who suffered and died and rose again. Knowing that did not erase the tears or mend my heart overnight, but it gave me somewhere to look when the waves crashed. I chose, sometimes minute by minute, to look up.

Grief, for me, quickly slid into something deeper. Getting out of bed felt impossible. My appetite disappeared. I would try to return to "normal," only to collapse under the weight of my son's absence. I kept replaying the night in my mind: the knock, the faces, the words. I wondered whether I could have prevented any of it: *What if I had said this? What if I had done that?* The questions were loud. The silence after them was louder.

In that early darkness, I also wrestled with God: *Are You here? Do You see me?* I learned that faith is not pretending you don't hurt; it is bringing your hurt to the One who can hold it. On the worst days I whispered, *"Help me, Lord. I'm not going to make it if You don't help me."* And somehow, breath by breath, He kept me.

I wish I could say the pain faded quickly. It did not. But I can say comfort began to appear in small ways: in a friend's text, in a quiet moment when the sobs slowed, in the certainty that God had not abandoned me. I was not the same woman I had been on September 23, 2017. I did not yet know who the "new me" was, only that I would have to find her with God's hand in mine.

What Helped Me

- **Name the day**. I used the full date, September 24, 2017, so my mind wouldn't keep saying "today" forever.
- **Breathe and hydrate.** When I couldn't eat, I sipped water and small broths. Surviving is holy work.
- **Accept help for logistics.** I let my children and relatives field calls and make initial arrangements so I could simply grieve.
- **Set gentle limits.** I answered only the messages I could. The rest waited.
- **Give grief a place.** I allowed time each day to cry and to pray, so tears didn't ambush me every moment.

Scripture to Hold

- **Matthew 5:4:** "Blessed are those who mourn, for they shall be comforted."

A Short Prayer

Father, I don't know how to live this new life without my child. Hold me when I cannot hold myself. Quiet the racing thoughts. Meet me in every breath with Your comfort. In Jesus' name, amen.

Arrangements

Planning for a loved one's funeral is heartbreaking. Making those arrangements for your child is a devastating and unimaginable pain. Andre's sisters and brother took on the responsibility of handling his service. There is so much more involved in arrangements than simply choosing a funeral home, church, and time.

My son had to be identified, then transferred to our hometown of Corpus Christi for the funeral. Our immediate family was in San Antonio, while Andre was in Houston. Thankfully, we had family in the Houston area who stepped in to help us. My niece went to identify his body, an extremely difficult task, I am deeply grateful I did not have to face myself. I often wonder where I would be today if it had been me.

Even now, I sit and think about this in disbelief:

Andre, I asked you not to buy that motorcycle, but you were determined to make your own decisions. You had no idea how much we still needed you, how much I long to hug you tightly again, or to feel your hands resting on my shoulders.

I saw the changes in you during those last days. I noticed the peace in your smile, though at the time I didn't understand it. Now I believe your heart had truly been changed for the better. Andre, I love you so much. I always will. You will never, ever be forgotten.

Guidance for Other Parents

If you are walking this road, know that the logistics will be overwhelming. Having family or trusted friends to handle calls, emails, meals, and details can be a lifeline. Some parents need to handle every step themselves to feel close to their child. Others, like me, find comfort in allowing others to step in. Neither way is wrong. Choose what keeps you standing.

During the service itself, remember: it is not about perfection. It is about love, remembrance, and faith. Allow yourself moments to cry, to rest, and to breathe. Once the service is over and the house grows quiet, that is when the hardest part begins. The silence, the thoughts that replay endlessly, those can be heavier than the arrangements themselves. Be gentle with yourself in that season.

What Helped Me

- **Delegating tasks.** My children and relatives took on phone calls, scheduling, and coordination.
- **Letting go of "perfection."** The service didn't have to be flawless, it had to be true to Andre.
- **Allowing rest.** I gave myself permission to step away and cry.
- **Remembering community.** I accepted food, flowers, and presence as gifts of love.

Scripture to Hold

- **Psalm 61:1–2:** Hear my cry, God. Listen to my prayer. From the end of the earth, I will call to you when my heart is overwhelmed.

A Short Prayer

Lord, this pain is unbearable, and these tasks feel impossible. Give me strength for the details and peace in the silence. Surround me with helpers when I cannot stand. Carry me when I am overwhelmed. In Jesus' name, amen.

Finding Yourself in the Midst

The service ended and I returned home. Family and friends went back to their daily lives. For about three months, I received phone calls and text messages checking on me and on Andre's sisters and brother. But what I remember most from that time was the unimaginable pain and the tears that would not stop.

I had no appetite for food and no energy to leave my room. Twice I tried to go back to work, but I couldn't manage it. Finally, I began counseling.

I found a Christian counselor, and during my first session he said, "Andre is here in the room now." Some might think those words are comforting, but to me they were the opposite. Don't feed me lies to ease the pain. Help me walk through this nightmare.

That night, as I lay crying into my pillow, I felt as if someone sat down at the foot of my bed. For several nights afterward, the same thing happened. My back was turned, and through my sobs I began talking to Andre. I also prayed, *"God, I'm hurting so badly. If You've allowed Andre to do this, thank You. If it's You, Lord, all praise to You."*

One night, as I wept in the dark, I felt what seemed like a hand on my back, as though someone was comforting me. At first, I thought of Andre and his long fingers. But deep in my heart, I came to believe it was an angel's feather brushing against me. What I know for certain is this:

God knew exactly what I needed, and He provided it. However He chose to provide that comfort, it was real.

Starting this journey without Andre was heart-wrenching. I lost interest in life as I knew it. I tried to busy myself by driving to appointments or running errands. I would watch the world moving around me; people busy, unaware that my world had stopped. No one knew the depth of my pain or how much my life had changed because of the careless act of a stranger who stopped suddenly in front of my son, causing his death.

I knew I had to forgive him. If I could not forgive, how could I expect forgiveness from God, who gave His only Son to die for me? God knows we are not perfect. He does not condemn us for anger or despair, but He does call us to release those burdens. If forgiving feels impossible, talk to God about it. Pour out your grief, your anger, your sorrow. He can handle it all.

I cried to the Lord, *"I know all this, but I don't know who I am supposed to be now."* The Pat before Andre's death no longer existed. I often asked myself, *Who is the new Pat?* I felt trapped inside a hollow shell, while some new version of me pressed against the walls of my heart, begging for release. I trusted that if I stayed in prayer, God would eventually set me free.

The crushing weight of sorrow made it hard to breathe. Just when I would begin to feel the smallest flicker of peace, grief would come crashing back.

Yet I held onto Scripture. One of the most powerful moments of Jesus' compassion is found at the tomb of Lazarus. He entered the grief of Mary and Martha. He wept. He showed us that mourning is natural, holy, and human. Each time sorrow overwhelmed me, I leaned on this truth: the Lord has not abandoned me. He understands my pain, my sadness, my struggle.

Walking this journey is difficult, but walking it without God is impossible. The "new me" will carry tears, but God is first in my life. I will persevere. I will survive. I place my life, and the lives of my children and grandchildren, in His hands.

What Helped Me
- **Letting God comfort me.** However He chose to, God met me in my darkest nights.
- **Being honest.** I told Him my anger, my confusion, my sorrow.
- **Facing forgiveness.** I chose to forgive, even when it seemed impossible.
- **Accepting change.** I admitted the "old me" was gone and asked God to help me discover the "new me."

Scripture to Hold
- **John 11:35:** When Jesus therefore saw her weeping, and the Jews weeping who came with her, he groaned in the spirit and was troubled, and said, *"Where have you laid him?"* They told him, "Lord, come and see."Jesus wept.

A Short Prayer
Lord, when I feel lost in grief, remind me that You are near. Help me forgive, even when it feels impossible. Show me who I am becoming in You. Hold me in Your arms when I cannot hold myself. In Jesus' name, amen.

Grieve Your Way

Grieving the loss of a loved one is very hard. I lost my father in 1989. He had pastored two churches, working tirelessly to preach the Word and provide for his family. He was strict, and I used to tell myself I couldn't wait to be on my own. My mother passed away in 2007. She was a woman of God; feisty and fashionable. She loved to dress up and even pushed Daddy to up his game. Losing both of them was heartbreaking, but I found comfort in knowing they were in the presence of God.

If I could go back in time, I would do many things differently. I would have asked God for wisdom and guidance earlier in my life. Perhaps I would have been more prepared for what was coming.

But nothing prepares a mother for the death of her child. Losing Andre was a pain unlike anything I had ever known. It opened my eyes as though I was seeing the world for the first time and all I could see was loss. The pain shook me to my core leaving me an empty shell. I tried to find my way back to "normal," but there is no normal after the death of a child.

I felt out of touch with the world. Laughter seemed foreign. I felt guilty for still being alive when my son was not. Yet I did not grieve as a mother with no hope of ever seeing her child again. I grieved as a mother who missed his voice, his hugs, his place at the table. What was I meant to do with this overwhelming emptiness? Was there still a "me" after this?

In the numbness I clung to my other children, because they mean the world to me. They deserved a mother who was present, loving, and whole, even when I felt broken.

Some people questioned how I grieved, or how long it lasted. But this is not their journey, it is mine. Everyone grieves differently. Some may have had time to prepare for a loved one's death through illness. They had chances to say goodbye. Others, like me, had no warning, no chance for last words. The anguish of a mother who suddenly loses her child is unlike any other.

Grieving is not learned from books, it is learned through experience. Good days and bad days will continue long after the loss. Yet parents who bury their children are among the strongest people I know. Grief affects not only your heart and spirit, but also your body. It takes every ounce of strength, and God Himself, to rise each morning and keep living.

By God's grace, the woman I was on September 24, 2017 is not the same woman I am today. Through His love and His presence, I have been changed.

What Helped Me
- **Accepting my own pace.** I stopped letting others dictate "how long" I should grieve.
- **Letting go of guilt.** I reminded myself that my children still here deserve a loving mother.
- **Naming the difference.** Losing parents broke my heart, but losing my son broke my entire sense of self. Admitting that helped me process it honestly.
- **Holding onto hope.** I grieve, but not as someone without hope.

Scripture to Hold
- **Matthew 26:38:** Then Jesus said to them, *"My soul is exceedingly sorrowful, even to death. Stay here and watch with me."*

A Short Prayer
Lord, help me to honor my grief without shame. Teach me to walk at the pace You give me, not the pace others expect. Lift the guilt from my heart and restore joy to my spirit, little by little. Thank You for holding me in every season. In Jesus' name, amen.

The What If's and Why

One of the hardest struggles in grief is the *"what ifs"* and *"whys."*

What if I had done this differently? What if I had been a stronger, more disciplined mother? Guilt creeps in, whispering that maybe I could have changed the outcome.

As mothers, we love, provide for, discipline, and guide our children. But as they grow, they choose their own paths. If they have been introduced to Jesus, they know Who holds their future. Even children raised in the best homes, with two parents and everything they need, can still wander. We cannot carry the weight of blame forever. If you gave your child your best, prayed for them, and showed them love, they knew they were loved.

In the early season of my grief, I often asked God, *"Why? Why my son?"* And in time I came to ask, *"Why not?"* So many mothers cry out in pain over the loss of their children. Some women I met in grief groups had lost two or even three children. One mother lost two sons in a single accident. Her pain was beyond measure. I pray for her often. Seeing her reminded me: my pain is real, but I am not the only one suffering.

If you are mourning and feel as though you failed your child, try writing a letter to them. Tell them everything you wish you could have said. Say the words you never had the chance to speak: *"I love you. I forgive you. I miss you."*

If you still have children here with you, take this opportunity to get it right with them. Pray for wisdom from the Holy Spirit. Call each of your children by name before God. Pray for them as they leave the house each day. Let them hear you say you love them.

Andre knew he was deeply loved. He and his sister DeDe often spoke about Jesus, and it gave me peace to hear them sharing their faith together.

Jesus suffered greatly for us. Though He had no sin, He hung on the cross so that we could be forgiven of ours. As His followers, we too will suffer.

If you have not yet accepted Jesus, know this: He died for you as well. Life and death are certain, but none of us knows the hour. Do not put off the most important decision you or your children could ever make. Introduce them to Jesus now. Fight for your children in prayer. When rebellion rises, never give up, stay prayerful. Satan waits for weary parents to stop praying, but a praying mother or grandmother is powerful beyond measure.

I have wrestled with rebellious children. I continue to pray, and I will not turn away. God has done, is doing, and will do more than I can see.

What Helped Me
- **Writing letters.** Putting my heart on paper to Andre gave me release.
- **Recognizing shared pain.** Hearing other mothers' stories helped me realize I wasn't alone.
- **Praying for my children daily.** I call each of them by name and place them before God.
- **Letting go of guilt.** I did the best I could as a mother; God knows my heart.

Scripture to Hold
- **Proverbs 18:10:** The LORD's name is a strong tower: the righteous run to him, and are safe.

A Short Prayer
Father, quiet the "what ifs" and "whys" in my mind. Heal the guilt that tries to take root. Remind me of the love I gave my child, and teach me to keep covering my children and grandchildren in prayer. Thank You for being my strong tower. In Jesus' name, amen.

Holidays, Anniversary, Birthday

Andre was killed on **September 24, 2017**, just two days before his 29th birthday and not long before the holidays. He loved Thanksgiving and Christmas, especially the food. Candied yams were his favorite.

That first Thanksgiving and Christmas, his siblings and I stepped away. We told the family we would spend the holidays by ourselves. Everyone is different, and for some, being surrounded by extended family is comforting. But for us, it was too fresh. Maybe I was being selfish, maybe I was still in the depths of depression, but I simply could not celebrate or be "happy." Before making that decision, I asked my children what they wanted, and together we agreed.

Each year, when Andre's anniversary passes, then his birthday, then the holidays, I can see how God has walked with me through it all. The first three years, I would drive off alone somewhere and scream it out. If I was home by myself, I screamed there too. Grief had to find its way out of me.

Now, nearly eight years later, those days are different. On Andre's birthday, I quietly say, *"Happy heavenly birthday."* Sometimes I can hardly believe my baby has been gone so long. Yet I also see what God has done with me and for me, and I cannot help but praise Him.

The anniversaries, birthdays, and holidays are no longer only sad occasions of longing. They have become opportunities to share memories of Andre with smiles and laughter. For this, I thank You, Lord. I trust You, God.

What Helped Me

- **Making space.** I gave myself permission to step away from holiday gatherings that first year.
- **Letting grief out.** Screaming in private gave my pain release when words could not.
- **Creating new traditions.** Now, we speak Andre's name, share his stories, and celebrate his memory with laughter.
- **Trusting God with time.** Over the years, He has turned painful anniversaries into moments of gratitude.

Scripture to Hold

- **Psalm 27:1:** The LORD is my light and my salvation. Whom shall I fear.

A Short Prayer

Lord, You know the weight that anniversaries, birthdays, and holidays bring. Teach me how to walk through them with both tears and thanksgiving. Fill the emptiness with Your presence, and turn sorrow into memories that bring peace. In Jesus' name, amen.

Prayer and Worship

At some point in grief, you must begin to care for yourself again. After losing Andre, I stopped. I neglected my health and barely ate. Eventually, I made a doctor's appointment. I had lost too much weight, and my doctor prescribed medication to help me regain strength. Little by little, I began eating real meals again.

I also returned to church, though I was fearful. Would I be overcome by grief? Would I collapse under the weight of it all? After service one Sunday, my pastor prayed over me and said he was *"praying death off me."* At that stage of my grief, I had given in to death. I didn't care anymore. It was selfish; I had three other children and grandchildren, but thinking rationally was not possible then.

Attending church was still hard. My emotions would spill over. Someone once told me not to grieve so deeply. I know the words were spoken in love, but I was hurting too much to receive them that way.

So I withdrew into prayer. I began talking to God every day: *"Help me, Lord. I'm not going to make it. I can't do this on my own."* Night after night, I poured everything out before Him: my pain, my anger, my despair. I wasn't letting go. I needed Jesus. The burden was too heavy to carry alone.

Step by step, tear by tear, He walked with me. He held the key to healing my heart and restoring my peace. Slowly, I began to breathe again. I began to thank Him for each new day.

His mercies, fresh each morning, carried me forward.

One night, as I lay in bed reading, I turned toward the wall. Clear as day, I heard: *"Jesus is taking care of you."* I whispered back, *"Thank You, Jesus."*

Another time, after reading at the park, I got into my car. As I turned into traffic, music filled the car, and a voice said: *"I heard your prayers. I answered your prayers. I know best, and he's with Me."* Tears streamed down my face as I praised God right there in my car. Some might not believe me. Some might think I'm crazy. But I don't care what anyone thinks, this was my encounter with the living God.

If you are praying for your child, keep praying. Never stop. God hears every prayer. I prayed many nights asking God to change Andre's heart and mind, and I believe He did. On July 24, 2017, at our last family gathering before his death, Andre apologized to cousins, aunts, and uncles he had hurt. He even mended his relationship with his father. I did not know any of this until the day of his funeral.

At the service, my pastor said: *"Mama Pat, your prayers may have saved your son."*

Mothers, grandmothers, pray for your children and grandchildren. Satan waits for us to grow weary and give up. Don't do it. Our children are worth every prayer, every tear.

God is good. He answered my prayers. Not in the way I imagined, but in the way He knew was best. For years, I struggled to believe this. I wondered if my prayers had led to Andre's death. But God opened my eyes. He owes us no explanation, He is God over everything. He changed Andre's heart and took him home to protect him from the evil to come.

I love You, Lord God, with all my heart, mind, soul, and strength. To You be the glory.

What Helped Me

- **Returning to church.** Even when it was painful, I allowed God's people to pray for me.
- **Daily prayer.** Honest, unpolished prayers carried me through.
- **Listening for God's voice.** In whispers and in music, He reminded me He was near.
- **Clinging to faith.** I refused to stop praying for my children, even when weary.

Scripture to Hold

- **Psalms 38:18:** The LORD's eyes are toward the righteous. His ears listen to their cry.
- **Revelation 21:4:** He will wipe away every tear from their eyes. Death will be no more; neither will there be mourning, nor crying, nor pain any more. The first things have passed away.

A Short Prayer

Lord, when I am too weak to carry my grief, carry me. When I am tempted to stop praying, strengthen me. Thank You for hearing my cries and answering in ways I may not understand but can trust. Keep my children and grandchildren covered in Your love. In Jesus' name, amen.

Understanding

Grief is like walking through the storm of your life. It raises questions you never thought you'd ask: *How did I get here? What did I do wrong? How will I survive this?*

I had never known such deep pain before Andre's death. For a long time, I wondered if I would make it. Grief will always be part of my life. Even now, years later, the ache is still present. But by God's grace, its grip has loosened. The sharp edges have softened.

I know I will carry this sorrow until the day God calls me home. But I can also see brighter days ahead. God has given me back my joy. I like myself again, as a mother, and as Pat.

Andre will always be remembered, loved, and missed. He is my baby boy. But I no longer feel guilty when I laugh. I no longer believe joy dishonors his memory. God has restored it to me as a gift.

When I think of Andre now, I remember that he is free. He is no longer caught up with the wrong crowd. He is no longer burdened by pain, rejection, or suffering. He is in the presence of God, fully known and fully loved.

To the grieving mother: keep your hand in God's hand. We know the pain, but we will come out stronger through the journey. We are not the same people we were before our child's death, but the new us can honor them in a different way. We can live in a way that makes them proud.

God has a purpose for each of us. Maybe it is to help someone new in their grief, maybe to walk daily with His Word, or maybe to share our ways of coping and surviving. Whatever it is, we give Him the glory.

What Helped Me

- **Accepting permanence.** Grief does not disappear, but it does change over time.
- **Allowing joy to return.** I learned that laughter is not betrayal, it is healing.
- **Remembering my child's peace.** Andre is free from pain, embraced by God.
- **Finding purpose.** God can use our journey to strengthen and comfort others.

Scripture to Hold

- **Psalm 23:1:** The LORD is my shepherd; I shall lack nothing.

A Short Prayer

Father, thank You for brighter days. Thank You for giving me back my joy. Help me to walk with purpose, to comfort others with the comfort You've given me, and to live in a way that honors my child. Keep me close until the day You call me home. In Jesus' name, amen.

In Closing

I hope you have been blessed by *A Mother's Journey*. My prayer is that you have felt encouraged, strengthened, and reminded that you are not alone.

Always pray for your children. Cover them daily with the blood of Jesus. The grief of a child is painful and unimaginable. How we survive it is not by avoiding the pain, but by walking through it day by day with Jesus beside us.

There is no shortcut, no way around it. But our Savior shares our pain. He wept at the tomb of His friend. He understands the broken heart of a mother.

So I declare today with boldness:
SATAN, YOU CANNOT HAVE OUR CHILDREN OR OUR GRANDCHILDREN.

We fight on our knees. We cover them in prayer. We trust the One who gave His life for them.

May God bless you on your journey. May He comfort your broken heart, restore your joy, and give you peace until the day you are reunited with your loved one.

Psalm 147:3: He heals the broken in heart, and binds up their wounds.

A Final Prayer

Lord, thank You for walking with me on this journey. Thank You for holding me through the darkest nights and for carrying me into brighter days. God bless every parent, grandparent, and loved one who grieves. Remind them that You are near, that their child is safe in Your presence, and that joy can return. We give You all the glory and praise in the highest. In Jesus' name, amen.

www.ingramcontent.com/pod-product-compliance
Lightning Source LLC
Chambersburg PA
CBHW031300120626
46545CB00007B/2911